MW01251866

Her Thoughts Her Words
ISBN:
Paperback
Copyrighted @2023 by Yougeeta Hansraj

FOR YOU

I dedicate this journey to my daughter, to my son and to my rediscovered self

PREFACE

This is my personal thoughts, and motivational quotes that helped me on
my road to self-rediscover after trauma and heartache.
Know that no matter the situation
NEVER lose yourself
but GROW from every situation that may arise.

In any journey too healing, know it is an emotional rollercoaster. You will
have great days and the next be upset and then sad. Just do not give up
on yourself as you are someone's prayer.

I hope you enjoy my rollercoaster back to still believing in love.

Her Thoughts

What is Real Love?

Is it the feeling you get...
when the wind whistles through the trees

Or is it the way the morning sun rises and warms your
face.
Is it the way the water gently washes the sand between
your toes?

Maybe it's the stillness of the sunset which reminds you of
a sense of peace.

You see, I want the peace, the stillness the sun rises and
sunsets.
But does it still exist.

Yougeeta Hansraj

Her Words

Time after time, time after time
I cried myself to sleep, while you laughed and
smiled at my expense.

Night after night I laid alone,
while you were out acting all wild with no care
for our home.

Day after day, you made me second guess
myself,
All because you were concerned about me
finding out about your true self.

You see the grass isn't greener on the other side.
Its greener when you water and maintain what
you have.

You knew what to say to get at me and to make
me stay.

Until enough is enough and myself worth is
more to me than you staying.

Yougeeta Hansraj

Her Thoughts

Do you take the pleasure in playing games with the heart.
Because so many have in the past

Or is it the feeling of an air BnB?
While searching for a home.

Is it knowing how I feel?
That makes you think it's okay to steal.

How is it that you feel peace and warmth?
When you are with me,
But can still entertain texts from another later that same night.

What if tables were turned?
That I was the one taking you for granted.
And left your heart stranded.

Just maybe if tables were turned.

Yougeeta Hansraj

Quote:

Certain storms are
unavoidable

Her Words

Yes, there are times, I want you back.
There are times I miss you.

Yes, there are times I question everything.
But then I remember
How you took me for granted and kept me out of sight.

The pain, so much pain you caused me.
Which caused me not to see clearly.

The countless nights I cried.
But I remained like I was paralyzed.

The days I praised you to others.
However, only to be let down by you.

You had a good woman a damn good woman.
But you, rather the trash that was left outside.

Yes, I may miss you,
but this heart that belonged to you no longer exists.
You can have them girls to fill your void for a moment.
But they can never compare to this woman right here.

When you realize that just give me my thanks quietly and know
What you once had was real, but you can never have it again.

Yougeeta Hansraj

Her Thoughts

Afraid to love.
Afraid to let go.
Afraid to feel.

All the stories of a broken heart
But still urn for the true thing

A love so true, you never want it to slip away.
A connection so electrifying it can light up the dark skies above.

A warm tenderness of true love that makes you melt like a hot summer day.

Will it be?
Can it be?

Yougeeta Hansraj

Quote:

It can not rain forever,
the sun will peak through

Her Words

Continuously trapped
between where friendship ends and where love lays.

Battling day in and day out if we should stay.
Should we say goodbye or continue this title less endeavour.

Because the thought of each other being with another.
For heavens sakes the sight of seeing each other with another.

Somehow, we always lead back to one another.

Are we renting this space in each other's hearts,
waiting for one of us to give the eviction notice?
Just to bury the other six feet under with their emotions.

Too afraid to retract, too scared to move forward.

Yougeeta Hansraj

Her Thoughts

I sit back and wonder.
Are you too afraid to acknowledge what this may be.

So now I hold back and stay still.

Are we just friends with benefits?
Or should we call it quits?

You see even if we call it quits.
Circumstances just lead us back to each other.

Too afraid to put a status on our situation.
But yet, uncomfortable seeing each other with another.

Because even in each other's absence our presence is still felt.
The comfort we have with each other.
Cannot be felt with no other.

The both of us denying our feelings but we both can't deny we care.
You see I like you, and I believe you like me too.
But too afraid to give it our all.

So where do we go from here?
Do we continue to break and mend each other's hearts?

Or do we give in and give it our all to this thing called love.

Yougeeta Hansraj

Quote:

Remember your not a contingent
with conditions

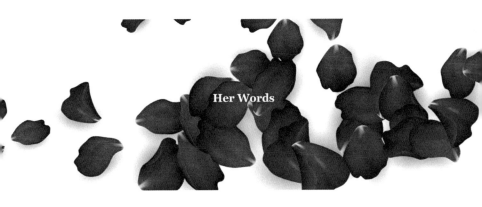

Her Words

Steady as a stream
But rough as the waves of the ocean.

Fighting with the current on which direction to go
Should I go with the current or fight back to where its safe.

Shhhh, close your eyes baby girl and feel the breeze as it glides in
your face.
Wait is that the subtle moment of peace or is it,

The urning for someone to say, "I don't want you no body but you."
"I want you to myself."

Yougeeta Hansraj

Her Thoughts

Can't believe I'm kicking with you the vibes be like them 90s R&B type
vibes relax cool chill maybe I should ask are you still down as
Jon B once did.

I want that Isley Brothers between the sheets type love.
One thing is for sure I don't want nobody, but you to make those.
Yo Train type night calls.

That type of vibe be when you see me out that makes you want to be like
Johnny Gill saying my, my, my.
Telling each other how we feel night and day as AL B Sure, sure did.

Finally ending each night by whispering in my ear you're my lady
that Freddie Jackson type of love.

This is the type of love I wait for.

Yougeeta Hansraj

Quote:

Don't have your tomorrows be robbed
by the mistakes you made today
Think wisely.

Her Words

You got your heart broken because you played offense for way too long
With your walls up, all you know is how to play defence.

Now that new love is here on the horizon and all you know is hurt.
Because you don't know you're worth.

Your worth is seen by many.
But you're blinded by the self-doubt.
Mentally battling.
Should you let love in or allow self-sabotage
and keep walking in this mirage.

Yougeeta Hansraj

Her Thoughts

Beautiful, talented, gifted strong.
Just not knowing it.

I was blind folded by
The one I thought I loved.
By the circumstances that surrounded me.

I was held hostage by the thoughts that were in my mind.
and which I started to believe
Is this real?

Then he came along, and my thoughts of self turned around.
His smile his sincere embraces warmed my heart.

His words caressed my soul as his touch lit a flame in mine.
His whispers of sweet words
The way he looks at me when our eyes connect.

The look, the feeling.
His soul embracing mine reminding me of nothing but good
things.
Breaking down barriers so deeply rooted.

A strong loving soul of a man reminded me that I am.

Beautiful, talented, gifted and strong.

Yougeeta Hansraj

Quote:

The version of me you created in your mind
is not my responsibility

Her Words

So why do I still worry about you till this day.
Cause you weren't loyal to me.

You were up when I was down.
You didn't share your love with me.
Your words did not meet your actions.

You used to tell me that I was always the one.
But you didn't care for me.
Again, your words did not meet your actions.

I put my trust in you.
But all you did was just lie to me.

So why do I still think about you?
When I know you're not right for me.
Why do you occupy my mind like I'm the landlord?
And you're the tenant paying rent?

Selfishly taking up space in my soul as if you were my mate.

You see I held you up.
You didn't care, you tore me down.

Continued.....

I saw your potential.
But you only saw my flaws, the very flaws you nourished
and then persisted to say they were the cause.

Things came to light.
But I was already in pieces
Crumbling inside of the very truth I had already known.

It wasn't me you see,
It was your battle within yourself.

It was you being a selfish human being.
Your own demons inside.

Your very own soul diminishing with every word you spoke.
With every breath that you took.

With every step you took
Till the day it became silent.

It was that day that I learned to breathe again.
Learned to feel again.
To see again.

Yougeeta Hansraj

Her Thoughts

Time.....

Time to be selfish for me.
Cause it's what I need.

It's time to hold me down.
Because the time is now.

I loved you and you couldn't hold on to that.

This is why it's my time to be selfish for me.
Cause it's what I need.

Yougeeta Hansraj

Quote:

You deserve someone that sees
you as someone too important
to lose.

Her Words

Now I know we are not a status.
But would you mind if I tell you that I want you for myself.

Late night calls and messages has been a thing.
But would you mind if I tell you I rather your touch.

Can I ask? Do I cross your mind when you're out with the guys?
Thoughts running through your mind as you pull up to the door.

Baby come through, lay down next to me leaving in the morning.
Wanting more.

While saying
You don't want nobody else but me.

Am I your first thought in the morning as the sun rises?
The last face you think of before you go to sleep.

Do you mind if I tell you I want no body but you laying by my side.

Yougeeta Hansraj

Her Thoughts

A love so desired.
A love just wanted.

A love so strong.
Its feels like an earthquake.

A love so bright.
That it shines bright as the morning sun.

A love that makes my legs weak.
A love of a king who can be my peace.

Pour into my cup and I'll pour into yours.
Let's overflow together.

A love where you want to stay together.
And not stray.

Where trust is no question.
A love that just flows.
But feels like the rapids.
Strong and uncontrollable

Just an ordinary old fashion type of love
So desired.

Yougeeta Hansraj

Quote:

Sometimes you can be so real and rare
that a person won't know how to handle it,
and they will mess it up before figuring it
out.
That's not on you.

Her Words

Had this feeling within.
That feeling that we would win.

You know my flaws.
I've seen yours
However; we remained.
Thought it all.

Then that day came
Where your true colours shined through.

I guess it was meant to happen.
Cause I gave you all of me.
Heart and soul.
But what I received was a bag of coal.

You took me for granted.
Cause I gave you my everything.
But you thought you would always have me.

Continued...

That I would never leave.
Your heartache changed me. It was something I had to feel.

Your façade masked by your private affairs.

My dream that turned into a nightmare
My pride crashing down.
Because you took everything for granted.
Cause you thought I would stay.

It all needed to happen,
Because of your betrayal
I'm better now.
Never to be taken for granted again.

Yougeeta Hansraj

Her Thoughts

Ignoring all those other guys who
are trying to get through the door
and wanting more.
Because your too busy noticing the
one who you want.

Patience wearing on your sleeve
But as the days continue to go by
Time is telling you that its time to leave
Torn.

Yougeeta Hansraj

Quote:

Don't be afraid to let them see the beauty that is within.

Her Words

Baby girl....

Let your femininity shine through.

Welcome that new love.

That love you so desire.

That, all that you need type of love.

Yougeeta Hansraj

Her Thoughts

Its times like this that which I am grateful.

Days like these I don't believe to be true.
Someone like you exists.

A person like you that my heart can't resist.

That a love like this still exists.
You're like every 90's love film come to reality.

It's your stare from across the room.
Your rich smile that makes all clouds disappear.

It feels like a dream, wait let me pinch myself to know its real.
Grateful that someone like you loves me like you do.

Yougeeta Hansraj

Quote:

Its okay, to start over and let someone else LOVE you the way your supposed to be loved.

Quote:

You have been tested and tried
time after time, and look at you
You're STILL standing.

Her Words

THE FINAL GOODBYE!

It feels so wrong that there are days I still think of you.
After all the years we were together.

There were days I wished you entered through the door.
But reality check.

Reality check because it was you who walked away.
I simply stayed quietly and watched the one true thing you
had slip away.
How did I allow you to waste my time.
How did I take what you put me through?

Day by day I drifted away.

Reality check in.
Memories of how you made me feel.
Alone and disconnected.
All the secrets you kept.

Continued...

Reality Check.
The tears you had me weep.
You were supposed to protect me.
But instead, you neglected my soul.

It took me some time.
But with time I realized I was like a phoenix, and I rose.
And you are a speckle of dust that I'm leaving behind.

Know this I am back with a vengeance every part of me feels
no love for you.

This soul is meant to be loved truly and whole heartedly.

I am letting......no let me rephrase this.
I must let you go.
So I can continue to prosper and grow.

GOODBYE.

Yougeeta Hansraj

Her Thoughts

There were days I really hated myself.
Struggling to love myself daily.
Couldn't see past the hurt I endured daily.

There were days I almost ended it all
Cause I thought it would be better off,
that I wasn't here at all.

You see, how much can one take?
Let down after let down.
Consistently like a clock, going round and
round.

He made me think that loving me was hard.
To the point, I wanted to end it all.

But it was my children you see, who saved me.
They showed me what real love was.
Looking at them reminded me of love.
Embracing me everyday.
Loving myself, and reminding myself of my true self
is what healed
me.
This is my TRUTH.

Yougeeta Hansraj

Quote:

Its time that you realize how
beautiful your soul is.
Let it shine so bright that they
can't help but notice.

Her Words

Dear Man,

I'm not looking for a man to make me complete.
But someone that is willing to take that leap.

Not someone to make me whole.
But someone who lights that flame in my soul.

Someone to cuddle with on the nights that are cold.
A man whose word will never fold.
A soul I can grow old with.

You see I want a partner with ambition.
Which together as one we can tackle life's missions.

I'm not looking for my knight.
But the one who is willing to try with all his might.

Yougeeta Hansraj

Her Thoughts

I know my feelings are not clear.
But know my intentions are real and I always want you near.

I know I'm not easy to read.
But know you give me something I didn't know I need.

Just the thoughts of you I can't resist.
Even when I try.
I can't stay away, I just want your kiss.

You're like the air that I breathe.
Breathing life into my soul with every breath
I take.

Your smile gives me light.
That light makes me smile even with the thought of you.

Your touch is something that I never thought I would experience
or feel.
You're like my man of steel.
Yes, my Superman.

Slowly but surely, you are letting these guards down with every
touch.
Every moment with every step we take.

It's becoming more of a sure thing.
I know I make it hard but understand.
You bring out the best in me.

Yougeeta Hansraj

Quote:

Take time to reflect and listen to within

Her Words

He's not just a man.

He's someone's home.
He's someone's peace.
He's someone's resting place.
He's someone's safe space in which they depend on.

And then....

She's not just a woman.

She creates his home.
She is his peace in which he seeks.
She's where he finds his comfort in his resting place.
It's her heart where he finds refuge.

Together they are each other's ONE.

Yougeeta Hansraj

Her Thoughts

On my single phase now
Not looking for anything

But you were that one.
That persistent one

Can't lie I denied every move you dished out.
I was the running back maneuvering from your every tackle.

I tried to diss you many times over.
Until later that night I realized you were someone I can chill with.

It continued through text making me wonder and
looking forward to what's next.

Reminding myself to take it slow.
But finding myself thinking about the day
I get to feel your warm embrace.

Yougeeta Hansraj

Quote:

Things will start to change
once you are willing to put the work into
IT.

Her Words

I've been searching for my king.
I may have found him.

His ex no longer has ties to his heart.
So, I know together our hearts can be painted on a canvas and it
would be a masterpiece.

Ladies, be finding him being to be a hundred.
But I'll add that Canadian tax
And have him double to a thousand.

You see I've started a new chapter in my life's novel.
And he may just be my life's piece that's been waiting to unravel.

I just may be his queen.
And he may just be my king.

So, let's build trust and loyalty.
And show the world what real love is made of
For what its' worth.

Yougeeta Hansraj

Her Thoughts

Soft, warm, Beautiful.
Finally, she is seeing a reflection of what was once lost.
A soul that was broken yet, you would never have known.
Finding peace within the broken reflection.
Finally, being put back together like a puzzle.

Leaving the one feeling she thought she needed.
Making the decision to water the version of herself
That was seeded and desperately trying to bloom.

Days go by and as she stares at the woman in the
reflection.
She finally makes the connection.

She has become the delicate woman she was before.
As she has found the person who she has been searching
for.
HERSELF.

But much more refined.

Yougeeta Hansraj

Quote:

You are rare.

Her Words

I think we stole each other's heart the first time we met.
The night our eyes first locked.

Now it's just us trying to see if it was an afterthought.

But you see it's like traffic on the I75 gridlocked.
Playing our favorite songs while stuck in traffic.

With every lyric that plays singing it out loud hoping
that we reach our destination.

Staring at you imagining that you can take me to another level
of love
that I've never experienced.

Trying to determine, if I should let you take the lead.
Wondering if I do, can you take us the distance.

Let's bare each other's reflection.
Therefore, we see each other's true intentions.

Yougeeta Hansraj

Her Thoughts

Maybe it's what I needed.
Maybe it's what you needed.
May be its what we need.

It's that smile that you have that lights up my face.
Maybe it's that connection we have.

We started off young.
As we grow it doesn't make sense why we haven't grown apart.

Maybe it's because we started off as friends the connection was
there.
We both moved on
Trying to move forward with other people less than each other.

Eventually it all leads back to the texts, it all starts to make sense.

Maybe it's that we are lost without each other.
Maybe it's our energy attracting one another.

Could it be that we started off young.
Could it be that we were friends.

Or just maybe it all leads us back to each other.
Cause it just makes sense.

Yougeeta Hansraj

44.

Quote:

The weight that is lifted , once you realize
your worth is everything.

Her Words

Why must the one's who are genuine
feel so much pain.

Feeling trapped with no escape.
Desperately trying to free myself.

My mind flustered.
It has me wondering what did I do wrong.

The thought of deception suddenly over takes me.
Feelings of needing to see.
See where this now takes me.

Yougeeta Hansraj

Her Thoughts

Never meant for this to happen.
You got on a flight.
Looking for experience.
Not expecting anything serious.
Now you're on short flight away.
To where he stays.

High up in the clouds.
A short flight away.
Sun Shining through the plane's window.
You already know.

He gives you that feeling of being a bonafide.
Making your connection justified.
Maybe its fate or maybe it was time just simply
waiting.
But for today,
You're on your short flight away.

Yougeeta Hansraj

Quote:

When your intentions are pure
You don't lose them, they lose YOU.

Her Words

All your attention.
That's what I've been craving.

I don't mind the Netflix and chill.
Just not tonight.

Turn off the lights.
So, we can lose sight in all we are about to do.

Create a bond so strong between us.
That it would be hard for anyone to try to break us.

Yougeeta Hansraj

Her Thoughts

Falling for you from a distance.

Here I am falling for you.
Your' every sense of being.

Talking to God about you.
Praying that you find solitude.

You see I knew I was falling for you that night
we first met.
Conversations sparked.

It was summer texts and conversations
I can not forget.

Hours apart but here you are taking up space in my heart.
You see, we can be something so beautiful and great.
Only thing is, that we are miles apart.

If you are meant to be mine.
Our souls will realign.

You see falling for you from a distance is a test.
But through my words I confess.

My heart can not wait till I am wrapped back up in your arms.
But here I am with miles apart
With you are taking up space within my heart.

Yougeeta Hansraj

Quote:

You are the blessing that someone has been asking for. Believe that.

Her Words

I don't know if it was fate.
But it took me meeting you
916 miles away while I was on a clean slate.

I met a King that night and it wasn't till after I felt like our souls
collide.

Our souls and minds align.
It must have been a sign of our energies
gravitating to one another.

I know you may have dark clouds.
But together I believe our light will shine through the darkness.

A king found
Here I am standing in front of you, letting you know as long as
you allow me in.
I promise to submit.

You see I already know how special you are.
Because everything is telling me that I am meant for you and
you are meant for me.

Let us both continue watering each others souls.
Igniting the flame which is in one another.
As to the reason we will both shine together.

Yougeeta Hansraj

Her Thoughts

May I have a moment of your time?
Because Babe, I want to tell you this just only one time.

I want you to be mine.
You're definitely my kind.

When I am around you,
I feel a different type of high.

When I'm in your arms I don't feel the ground.
It's like your embrace takes me to paradise.

Put your lips onto mine.
You are always on my mind.
Just want to be by your side

Lay with you side by side
All night long.
Embracing your body next to mine.

Now that I have taken your moment in time.
What do you say

Can you be mine?

Yougeeta Hansraj

Brown Skin Man

I just need to let you know.
You are brilliant and you are strong.
It shines through everyday.

The way you walk through the door and carry
yourself in that certain way.
No wonder they are intimidated and uptight
around you.

You deserve your flowers too.
You carry the weight of the world on your
shoulders, and God knows that its not easy
thing to do.
But I want you to know with me, your Queen
you have a safe space.
So inhale and exhale, your mind and heart is
safe with me.

You deserve to be honoured and loved.
And I'm just here to let you know I see you
Brown Skin Man.
Thank you, for all that you do.

Yougeeta Hansraj

Her Thoughts

A Letter to our Men

Grey clouds hovering over.
Thoughts racing through your mind,
like a never ending marathon.
One thing after another.
Slowly breaking you down day by day.
Leaving you feeling,
like a wrecking ball hitting you like a ton of bricks.

Like no other braving each and every day
with a smile wondering when someone
will ask you
Are you okay?
Our Princes and Kings know this!
Its okay not to be okay.
Because many of us are not, at the the end of the day.

You say, your okay
But that's not what you really mean.
Just having the urge of just wanting to be seen.

Your days maybe feeling
As like cement brick weighing you down in the sea.
Just trying to make it to the top to breathe.
Know its okay not to be okay today.
But know this
I'm here to ask you
How are you today?

Because there are days all you can do it walk by faith.
But know this after every moon, the sun rises.
And with that this reminder.
There is so much more to live for.
And I know you know this at your deepest core.
You can rise above it all.
And know its okay not to be okay today.

Yougeeta Hansraj

Quote:

The heart she has, the love
she gives, the loyalty she
lives by is real.
AND..that is rare these
days.
But she won't beg to be
chosen.
She will go where she is
celebrated.
MEMEKing

About the Author

Yougeeta who resides in Ontario, Canada is a mother of two.
She is the daughter of a Trinidadian mother and a Guyanese father and
a middle sibling.
A Domestic Violence survivor, when life got rough, she found an outlet
in writing to express herself.
As life continued, she has worked as an Events manager, and currently
works in the healthcare industry.

With society today it is easy to get caught up, life, love and unexpected
turns.
Yougeeta most proud moments thus far is being a mother, an aunt and
now experiencing being a grandmother to an amazing little boy whom
she calls her gummy bear.

These thoughts and words is the most vulnerable that Yougeeta has been.
She hopes that these words demonstrates that no matter the situation you
have been dealt, you can still believe in a everlasting love.
LET YOUR BEAUTY THAT'S WITHIN SHINE BRIGHT.

Manufactured by Amazon.ca
Bolton, ON

38086763R00040